EMOTIONAL PARALYSIS

PHASES OF EMOTIONS

VANDANA

ISBN 979-888546513-7

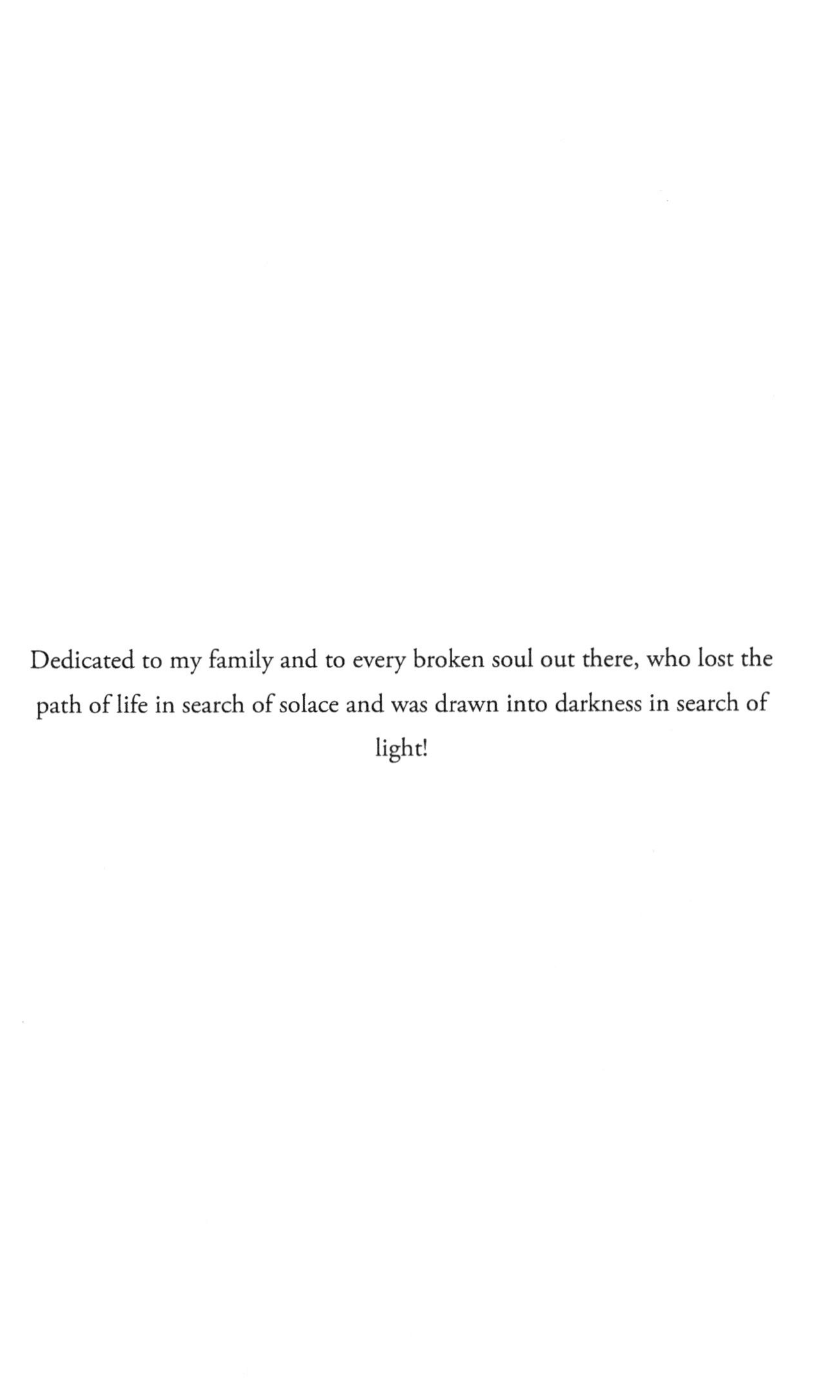

Dedicated to my family and to every broken soul out there, who lost the path of life in search of solace and was drawn into darkness in search of light!

Contents

Contents

Acknowledgements

The journey of writing this book has really been enthralling. I would like to thank my brother for supporting me and helping me in making my manuscript.

I would also like to share my word of gratitude to the Notionpresspublishing team for providing such a great opportunity to emerging writers into authors.

I would also like to thank my mother for suggesting me different ideas and for patiently dealing with my mood swings while I writing this book and preparing its existence in the book world!

Also, I would like to thank google and Pinterest, etc for the illustrations and art I have used in my book as they have enhanced the beauty of this book.

Part-1: Love and heartbreak!

1. You came and left!

You did exactly what I'd supposed,
Within a few days, you came and proposed!
You had changed my life,
and I was thinking to be your bride!
I told you it was an attraction,
But you wanted to build a connection!
I warned you it won't last for days,
You promised to manage the ways!
Now, what about your words,
You end up breaking my trust.
I am left with my uncared dreams,
and too with my silent screams!
You shattered my heart,
and proved that you had no heart!
Now I have to accept,
Rather than expect!
Life is cruel,
and love is brutal!

✶✶✶✶✶

"Profit and loss are nothing more than the illusion created by humans' unnecessary desires!"

2. Jolly to gloomy!

I was a happy person,
The reason of was is gloomy!
I had lost my charm,
The day you said goodbye!
I was standing near your carcase,
Reminiscing our past,
Gazing you and stars,
I was perturbed and,
It took me a while,
To get on my nerves
that I have lost you!
My eyes oozed the moment,
I got a thought of you!
You were a star,
Who shined us all,
With hope and love!
The journey we had spent,
Was the most spectacular!
The distance we had covered,
Was the most intriguing!
You took my hand with love,
And helped me to tackle my
adversities!!
You are missed every morning,

You are loved every night!
I can Perceive your spirit
Even in disguise,
I can discern your presence
Even being so distant!
You and I were never the two souls,
You took my half with you,
And my smile disappeared
with moon!
Our heart and vitality are still connected,
That's the reason you were never dead!
You always filled me with gaiety,
Every morning I woke up with you
And that too with woes,
the moment I took on my senses
And comprehended the same feeling
That I lost my star!
But my dear,
You are alive, in my thoughts,
wandering in my fantasies,
And the reality in my dreams!

✶✶✶✶✶

"Love sees no bar, love has no protocols,

Love endorses a war, love acknowledges all!"

3. My life is yours!

Am I breaking your heart?
Am I being too selfish?
Am I being too messy?
Am I being too carried away with my ego?
What am I?
What am I doing?
My SELF is facing crises
For the different ideologies
Between my fantasies and reality!
I don't want to hurt you
This is a clear speculation!
I don't want to lose you
This is my pretty explanation
For all my pointless stuff!
I love your presence exactly

the way you want to Love me!
I am bounded sweetheart,
With my own challenges!
I am restricted with my
past mistakes and flaws!
I wish if I could able to give you
The love you deserve for!
I wish if I could be with you
For the time we have together!
You are a child, I want to care
You are a sweetheart, I want to
Protect!
I don't want to spoil our equation
For this so-called term relationship!
I care about your thoughts
I care about your odds
I care about your emotions!
I like the way you link our
destiny!
I like the way you smile
When you see me!
Why are you so cute?
I can't resist me thinking of you!
I miss you but I am afraid to tell you
I have so many emotions for you
Hiding in my heart and soul,
But I am scared to let you know!
I don't know if we could stay like this
FOR-EVER!

VANDANA

I don't know if we are meant to be
TOGETHER!
what I know is you,
What I care for is your
Lost smile!
If our story has written in a
different way,
I would love to see the plot twists!
Our journey may not be written
Together, but my life is yours for
The remaining years!

✲✲✲✲✲

"Beautiful things never take place with prior information;

they just happen and fill our lives with joy and happiness!"

4. You in my life!

Talking endlessly about ourselves
To gazed at each other secretly,
I always hid my blushing face
So that you can't see!

*****

My memories with you were real,

My perception of you was clear!

My decisions went wrong,

But my intention was pure!

You and I both have failed in many ways,

But together we will make them pave!

Your parting smile pierced my heart,

Your utter words shattered me apart!

But even though the separation,

Can't stop you in my imagination!

Our relationship status might have Changed,

But our emotions are still the same!

Let's start a new bond,

And conquer our fate beyond!

5. Just say it!

You're never meant to me
Then why do I always think of you
I am driving crazy for you
Can't you see my happiness
When you and I hang out together
It's just not friendship you consider
It's more than that,
I can see in your eyes
Then why do you try to hide
Just say it, for once
For once just say it!

You like me, I like you
Isn't it the confession time?
Why have I been so messy
To spoil things for you too
My heart gets flutter every time
I see you!
Were we destined all along?
Or am I just dreaming!
You were always in my thoughts
And now in my words,
I have fallen for you
And what about you?
Just say it, for once
For once just say it
You love me, I love you
Isn't it the confession time?
You are so far ahead
I want to hug you
And feel the presence
Of your livelihood!
Your memories make me
Feel sad, I want to cry
On you and would love to feel your
Speedy heartbeats, your perfume still
Hides within my senses!
Should I hold back or split it out
What have I been going through?
Can you please promise me to
Stay always in my fantasies

VANDANA

If not in my realities!
Just say it, for once
For once just say it!
We have been dating
It is the party tonight!

6. Juliet and Romeo

That we all could take a hand
They sacrificed their life
To obliterate the hatred
The story forced to end their families
That violent feudal crept and taken their life!
The heroes of joy,
The heroes of pain!
The warriors in fantasy,
The warriors in reality!!

"Prioritize your heart,

you'll never fall apart!"

7. Where were you?

You miss me,
But I don't belong
to you anymore!
You lost me the
day when I was
crying for you
and you left me
at the cafe,
Without replying!
I heard you said
you miss the bond
we shared!
But what did you do?
to protect our bond??
Where were you when
I needed you the most
Where were you when
I was dealing with anxiety
And questioning my discretion
Where were you when
I was healing the scars
you gave me as a present!
Why do you care for me?
all of a sudden, after all

You used to think
of me as a burden!
I appreciate that
after all this time
you realised my worth
However, you lost me
You lost us
FOREVER!!

*****

8. That monsoon night!

Walking together over Street,
Far away from lies and deceit!
Holding hands tightly,
Twinkling at each other brightly!
The serenity in the breeze,
And those stalking trees!
Gazing him and stars,
Away from all the repellent scars,
To being in presence of his,
I was ready to discard my wings!
With all those passing thoughts,
I wished him with my fingers crossed!
Suddenly, a voice got my heed,
And my breath got on speed!
Clouds were wickedly thundering,
And my notions were blooming!
With that frightening facial look,
I clutched his shirt and felt brook!
Held him so tight, leaving no space,
I could hear his beating heart pace!
With this, a heavy downpour drenched,
He grasped my waist and wrenched!
Pulled my face and kissed my forehead,
The beautiful remembrance he laid!

Tears Cascaded from his eyes,
When he hugged me for the first time!
Glittering eyes of him,
Made my heart skip a whim!
Appraising two joyous souls,
Beneath the shades of the moon!
Nightingale singing jovially,
the melody tune!
The symphony of the nightingale
and the drizzled of rain,
Soothed our vigorous pain!
That enchanting night,
Brought our lonely world
Into light!

*****

"The love we share with that certain someone is unique and beyond every conjecture!"

9. Life was good!

Life was good when we were together!
Life was good when we were immature!
Life was good when we had no phones!
Life was good when I used to write letters,
And you kept them in your heart!
Life was good when memories were real,
And reverie was imaginary!
Life was good back then,
Please take me back to you!

10. My first notion!

When I saw you, I saw my other half,
When I looked into your eyes, I saw the depth of loneliness!
When I scrutinized your soul, I found deep wounds in it!
You and I might not be the perfect individual person,
But our combination was the most positive and vibrant!

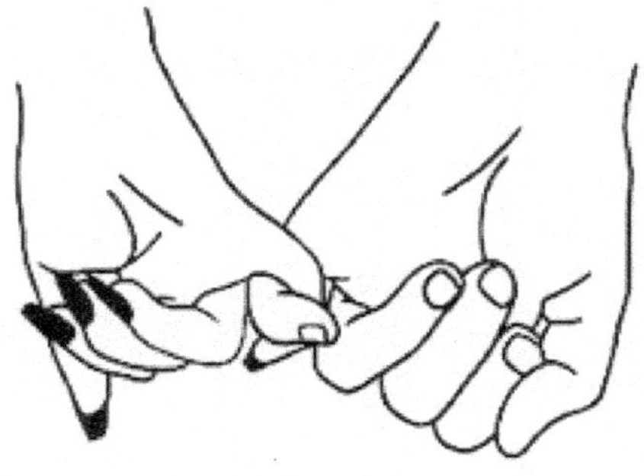

*****

"All our thoughts hold the depth,

But certainly not the whole truth!"

11. Before falling!

Before falling in love with me
You should know some facts,
I may look mature to you,
But deep down, a child is hidden!
I may appear an attitude bitch,
But I am soft-hearted and never going to ditch!
I may look sophisticated and smart,
But believe me, sweetheart I am just a brat!
My list of interest may be a bit longer,
But qualities in choosing a partner is none!
I may not share my thoughts with you,
But the thoughts I care about is of you!
I may be good at words,
But trust me I go blank,
When I am in front of you!
My idea of love is quite distinctive,
But my way of loving is interesting!
Hence saying this all,
Is a reminder call!
People appearances can be deceiving,
And their interior can be amazingly contradicting!

*****

12. Long-distance Relationship!

When we were together in real,

Things were definite and clear!

You loved me with your whole heart,

And assured me that we will never get apart!

Those beautiful letters you used to write,

Made my heart joyous and delight!

When you used to embrace me with kindness,

And used to bruise my hair to harbour all my weakness!

All those memories are now part of me,

They made my heart smile, can't you see?

In this pandemic, we were left with no choice

And started our new journey with rejoice!

The journey of a long-distance relationship,

And the hope of strengthening the ship!

I used to smile whenever my notification had your name,

And it led my heart to bloom with burning flames!

One month passed on a happy note,

But what's next about to happen, I was completely unknown!

Suddenly one day,

You said something you wanted to convey!

You wanted to end the commitment,

And when I raised my disagreement!

You shouted over me without my consent,
And forgot the days we together have spent!
I was pleading in front of you,
But you ignored all my woes!
Everything changed in a moment,
And it was the last time we have spoken!
I never thought things would go this tragic,
I still yearn for Almighty's magic!
For being a part of each other, in every phase of life,
Admiring each other flaws patiently to cultivating fuss and strife!
Everything has changed now,
Priorities got changed by thou!
I wonder, what might have happened,
That made our connection dampened!
Am I really this bad to you,
Or you got someone else, huh?
I thought even if we date virtually,
Things won't go this brutally!
I never imagined you would break my heart,
And perish my sentiments to break the spark!
The scars you have given to me,
It Will remain forever embedded in my soul, you see
I have buried all the remembrances of thee,
And vow to never change my status to we!

✳✳✳✳✳

"Losing you was not my decision,

Loving you was never my intention!"

13. Emotional instability!

Fight against my endless solitude
That is making my life crude!

• 52 •

Part-2: Existence and Brutality

14. Different Orientation: A bliss!

One very fine day,
Darkroom and sky were grey!
I woke up in an Oblivion,
And was frozen with delirium!
Everybody was gazing at me
like a cursed moon,
And remarking me in a bad tune!
My identity as a transgender was revealed,
And that opened which was concealed!
It was an unacceptable truth,
Should I feel sad or ruth!
I was startled by those staring eyes,
It was nothing but an awful surprise!
Lying there I was questioning my entity,
And my heart was filled with anxiety,
To whom should I ask the reality?
Is it my deficiency or god's divinity!
I was looking at my mother,
And my soul was in shudder!
She was howling while looking at me,
All the denunciation can be seen!
Seemed to be my life had no worth,

My existence couldn't be changed by the birth!
This is who am I,
There's nothing to be shy!
If this world is discordant,
I will not bear more torments!
With my head down,
I made a vow,
And left my house,
In search of solace!
Stepping out in this world,
I realize the hunger and wrath,
In the eyes of humans, unfurled,
Making me question my path!
I was disheartened into pieces,
When my parents denied my acceptance,
And hence my tears drenching my soul
Increases,
Cutting down my soul in abundance!
Walking and walking barefoot,
All night pared my skin-root!
My existence is full of colours,
Like the shimmer of valour!
What if I am different?
My capabilities are magnificent!
What if my choices are not the same?
To love and to live is my absolute aim!
While stepping every mile ahead,
I was counting the blood droplets I'd shed!
Till now, tears were all drained out,

And my voice was ready to shout!
Shout against the devil act,
Of not accepting the community,
Of different orientation facts,
That shows a lack of empathy!
But What if this world has lost it's
Faith in humanity,
I will raise my voice to amplify,
The importance of this community,
And eventually, it will soar high in the sky!

"I wish if I could go to the other world,

The world full of acceptance and admirations!"

15. Dear Open Sky!

When I look up to the sky, I see freedom and equality.

Sitting underneath your shelter make me feel better and blessed.

You work as a parasol and insure me with your presence.

You admire my odds and evens and support me in my adversities.

You brighten my life by harbouring sun in your wide arms and sparkle my tears as shining pearls by giving wings to the stars.

Whenever I feel desolate, you empower me with your warmth refuge and soothe away my all worries.

I wonder, what are you in particular, do you also have emotions like us (jolly, melancholy, anxiety, insecurity, grief), what is your place where you live?

How it feels like to be above us and scrutinizing every phase of our life.

Do you laugh at us or feel pity when we become helpless to encourage our own will?

The open blue sky, serene and elegant, whereas the dark sky is full of stars, eerie and profound.

Your enchanting composure and dazzling appearance lighten my whole day.

Open sky, a place where there are zero comparisons and zero excoriation, and full of veneration.

I want to fly in that open sky relinquishing all my despairs and dreads.

I want to be a part of you, a tiny little droplet aside by you and wants to be far away from this world full of hatred and criticism.

I wonder do you also have heartbreaks and if so, does it symbolize rain?

You know I have myriad questions to ask and you have patience ears.
I wish to be a part of you, I wish to be known to you.
" Dear open sky"!!!

16. Childhood: Collection of memories!

The last time I lived to the fullest were the days of my childhood, where I used to sleep without worries and smile for real, not to fake my emotions. Those days had the power to brighten my dullest times and to sway all my tensions.

In childhood, innocence was our part of life and guilt had no space.

Where we used to care about one another and were far away from lies and deceit.

Where friendships were real and relationships were reverie.

Where we had the liveliest vitality and happy hearts.

Where dejection and desolation were unknown to us and being loved and happy is what we knew. Where there was no anxiety in our souls and no expanse for "dilemmas of depression".

Where we had no insecurities to lose someone and had no responsibilities of work.

Where we can play for almost an entire day without worrying about the future.

Where Emotions were incoherent and the heart was subtle.

Where there were zero controversies and zero conspiracies, where " I'll never talk to you" was temporary and melancholy was skedaddle.

Where people used to show real faces and never disguise their true vibes.

Those days were indeed magical, where we used to sleep over our mother's lap, where true peace finds its way towards us.

Where we used to wander recklessly around playgrounds.
Where real interaction used to happen in reality and not over phones.
Now that time has long gone and we are left with the good memories we
shared and the quality time we had with our favourite peers.
While writing this all, my eyes are sobbing and my hands are quivering, I
miss the time where that wide smile showed all the teeth, I used to wear
all the time without any worry of judgments. It feels so nostalgic and
worth writing!

＊＊＊＊＊

"If there is love,

there is fear

Fear of losing the love!

If there is fear,

There is realization,

And realization comes along

with acceptance"

17. Accept the difference!

I am skinny not a piece of wood,
I can take care of myself and you also should!
I eat, I drink why should I give you a proof,
To people who body shame, yes, I am aloof!
I will wear sleeveless, who are you to judge,
I will wear shorts with thinly legs, stop
This unnecessary fuss!
Objectifying my body and shaming me down,
Telling my flaws without my consent, I'm not
Your pawn!
If I am skinny, that's my choice!
If I am fat, it's my rejoice!
My belly may be a little round,
Meddling with my discretions
Sieve my heart with many wounds!
"Humiliating people

And harassing is illegal
Their ruthless comments
Breaks down the commitments
One made to oneself
Just because society is full
Of themselves!
Put some weight,
You'll look great!
Do some exercises,
You can alter your
recognises!"
All your expectations
Appear so meaningless,
Whatever is given to me
I feel proud and bless!
If my height is small,
Why is it your downfall?
If I am a heightened person,
What makes your health worsen?
If my complexion is dark,
Appreciate it instead, you bark!
My success doesn't depend on my colour,
My Downfalls needs to be enriched with valour!
If I am a Muslim, does it make me less patriotic?
My love for India is bounded if it sounds exotic?
If I am Slightly different from the societal norms,
Then unite and support the change, the laws must reform,
To halt the chaos being created by the idealistic mentality,
That vandalise victim's sentiments to depravity!

The utter words, spoken from the society,
Filled my heart with uncertainty and anxiety!
Stop putting restrictions that belongs to me,
Stop oppressing me and let me free!
My different shape and size,
Depicts my unique side!
Take actions against this catastrophe,
And celebrate the difference happily!

*****

"I ponder, if my dilemmas can be unfurled

And can solace my burning sensation!"

18. Dilemmas of depression!

I don't feel like talking anymore.
Can I become what I was before?
I want to isolate myself from all
the stuff going on around me,
And to remain in my bubble and
never get out of it, so that none can see!
I ponder, what if I someday disappear?
no replies, no more attending calls,
no more my insane talks to hear!
Will someone miss me?
Will anyone try to find out about me?
Will any of the soul cry for me?
I wonder, to what extent
will they strive for me?
This is not the end of what I think,
I have myriad dilemmas that surround
my mind every day like the clink!
I am tired of being kind,
I am drowsy of being always available
for people that destroy my mind!
People never consider asking me
if I am okay or not!
And this unease feeling makes
my heart distraught!

People often adore me by saying
that I am way too good in words,
But how do I fill the void of my heart,
That has been fallen apart?
Irrespective of my efforts!
With all the broken pieces,
I smiled and made them seize!
I admire when they compliment
And my heart starting to flutter,
But I am exhausted from speaking
too much where my voice is
unheard and my soul is dying in shudder!
I, always try my level best to calm people's
pain with my soothing phrases,
but what about the anguish
my heart is withstanding for ages?
What about my unhealed scars?
that leads to inflicting wars?
Do people still care about my opinions?
Do people still question my silence?
Is it depression or a mere nightmare?
Dreadful nights with oozing stares!
Stop enforcing the smile to fake,
It's okay now, to glow for our sake!
Loneliness has now become a part of me
No matter where I go, how much I run,
I always find its oddments for free!
How paradox, I feel so desolate even
though an ample amount of people

surrounds me.
I feel abandoned, even after
putting in so many efforts,
yet nobody sees!
Am I this complicated or
you don't want to know
what is beneath my soul?
I am suffering emotionally,
Dealing my senses with no control!
This unnecessary anxiety
you have given me as a present,
is killing me deep down.
Depression is a serious mental
trauma,
Subjugating souls, leading to melancholy
"People often consider it as a drama"!
And show their act of irresponsibility
and folly!
Some fight and triumph in defeating
this illness,
but some succumbed and eventually die,
And all the waves of laughter and pain
ends in emptiness,
And tears Cascaded from the sky when they
Say 'GOOD-BYE'!
It's not the victims' fault when they
Yield to depression,
but rather the people who don't believe
and support the victim.

There are many people
who are facing and fighting
this dreadful illness.
And despite this eerie dilemma
They never flinch and bear with stillness!
In this era of science and technology,
where people can take care of their
loved ones even sitting miles apart,
They do not even prefer talking
with heart!
We are so busy pleasing others
while forgetting about the person
sitting next to us,
causing waves of solitude thus!
This is so unfortunate that
We are immensely involved in showing
and accepting facades that we
forgot about our real side.
The ideology of being perfect
made us so coward that we feel
dishonoured to show people our bad vibe!
We are struggling so hard to be someone
Who's completely different from what
we are actually in person,
And so busy in simulating perfect hues,
that we failed to appreciate the flaws
that truly makes us flawless verses!

"Drowning into blooming flowers, and dying with shining stars!"

*****

"No doubt the world is enduring so much and it needs to be rebuilt, I believe that the crucial part of healing the world is to obliterate the ill mentality of people regarding rapes and prostitution."

19. Utter words of her soul!

Screams, havocs, anguish,
She was tantalized by three men,
And left on the street to languish!
Humanity is at depravity again!
She was unable to breathe,
And her soul was shuddering,
Delinquency in the city,
hypocrites seethe!
Witnessing her shorts,
Everybody was judging!
Blood splashes were
everywhere around the floor,
Her vagina was badly shattered,
Her beliefs were at war,
And her fantasies got battered!
Lying there, she was questioning,
The world creation of divinity,
Tears drenched from her eyes,
She was perturbed and trembling!
The fear of witnessing others,
In the same situation, she was that day
Sieved her heart in many ways!
To witness this heinous act,
Is not only traumatising for the victim,

But for every girl, who can understand
The agony and suffering of her!
She wondered,
Will our government take actions
Against the perpetrators,
Or ignore her like they always do?
Will people stand by her side and
Support her if she dies, or they'll
remain quiet holding their woes?
Will people going to criticise her
For her dark lipstick,
Or they going to see her
Worth irrespective of this?
The Society will soon pass over her too,
By saying" just another rape case"!
And when the authority has failed to
Defend them, then what can we do?
Irrespective of all the dilemmas,
She whispered in God's ears,
"Please entrust me with one power",
She wanted to show that girls are not Coward!
The power which she wanted is to manipulate,
People mind with positivity,
And wanted to obliterate the levity!
This world needs to be free from hatred,
Then only it can heal and become sacred!
With these parting words,
She died, enshrined!

You called me your Queen
but then made me cry

*****

"People avoid being responsible,

And unknowingly support the impossible!"

20. Your Portrait!

Why things always happen,
In an unexpected manner!
Where we lose hope,
We get a ray of sunshine!
Where we need love,
We get heartbroken!
This world is full of lies,
This world is full of facades!
Inaudible screams,
Unhealed traumas!
Smiley faces,
Depressing eyes!
What on Earth is happening
With our young youth,
Stepping into the fake world,
And turning away from the truth!
There's not a single night
Where we don't wet our
Clothes and pillows,
Where we don't yell to our
loneliness and pray to quit
Our mere existence!
We succumbed for our Rights,
We forgot about self-love,

Out casting our Worth,
Failed to appreciate our flaws!
We independent people, depending upon
Others for our happiness!
My words aren't to hurt you,
My words aren't to de-frame your
Feelings and sentiments!
It's okay to be someone's reason to smile,
It's okay to be someone's favourite person,
But it's not okay to lose yourself in
Order to imitate the person they want!
It is not acceptable to only appreciate your
Smooth petals but not your deadly thorns!
To me, every person has their own portrait
It may be dark, maybe bright, may
Be the scariest and maybe the loveliest!
Just remember every portrait has a
meaning and has its beauty!
Let give the right person a chance to
Look into it!
And the day you'll find out your right soul,
You'll rejuvenate into a beautiful flower with
Thorns that are now acceptable and appreciable!

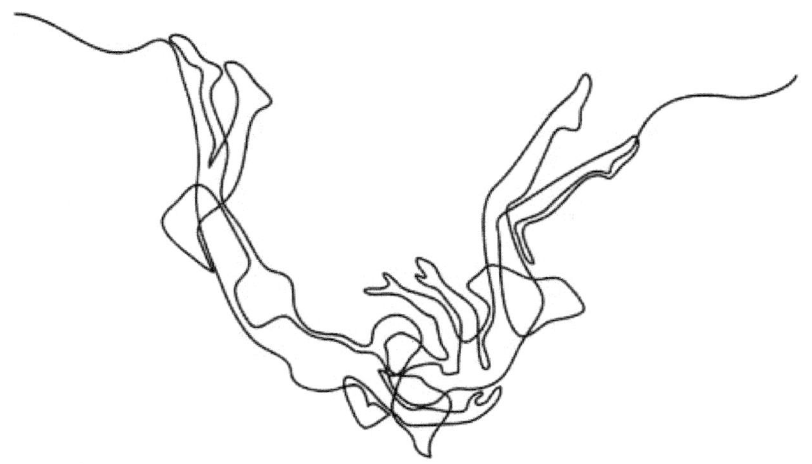

"Your existence gave me hope for light!"

*****

21. A Girl!

A girl full of enthusiasm,
A girl full of wildness,
The craziest girl
You will never encounter!
A girl full of positivity,
A girl full of self-esteem,
The most loveable of all
Then why is she alone?
Why there's an emptiness
In her heart!
Why her soul feels heavier
Every night!
Why her eyes are always
Swelling!
From where she has come
To where she lives!
Every mind is puzzled
With these questions!
Her personality varies from
Situation to person!
But what is she in person?
Is the most frequent asked
Question!
Every one of her colleagues

Is unaware!
A girl who admires night
More than the sunshine!
A girl who appreciates stars
More than moonlight!
Who keeps her desires in a shell?
Rather than opening up to the world!
Her eyes are oozing with blood
Her heart is breaking into parts!
Her past has many scars left
On her body and mind!
She is suffering emotionally
She is dealing physically
She failed, she triumphs
She tumbled; she rose!
She is the most gallant
And courteous person
I ever saw in my life
And got inspired by her!
Life sometimes out-casts us,
Breaks us, and then rearrange
Those broke parts and
Pour out a whole new version
Of ourselves!
"Watching someone smiling,
Doesn't always mean they are
Actually happy!
Watching someone crying
Doesn't always mean they are

Actually in pain!
You can't judge a person by
Mere looking,
We, humans, are the trickiest
Creature God ever created!
We laugh to hide the pain
We cry to hide our weaknesses!
We gain trust to betray,
We support to destroy!
There are dilemmas and mysteries
Hold beneath the human soul
But she is the master of all!

22. Eleiyaca's soul to stars!

Hey stars, doing well?
I'm right underneath your shelter
Admiring my odds and evens
I wonder, what if I could be one
The same as you, close to all
Affair to none, seeing all from
The above, laughing, crying, yelling
And helpless to encourage their own will!
I wonder,
How compelled we all have become!
This place, as serene as a turbulent
And as wonderful as an eerie
There is neither comparison nor
competition,
Full of veneration, zero excoriation!
Blimey! How fascinating!
Well, who am I?
Am Eleiyaca Dazura, a wayfarer!
Garrulous, always talk to me
like a rave!
I'm not banausic, not selfish,
It's that I'm too much what I'm not!
Stars! you know my life
Sitting above, scrutinizing all

VANDANA

I'm tired of being alive
In this world of fake people!!
I m a refugee, and you
How kind!
Providing your dark refuge!
To protect me from pain and sorrow,
I have left with devoid hopes,
Still struggling to get one!
Why am I even alive?
Why even am I struggling?
With my darks and dreads,
It seems like I had lost my
all strength,
And feeling like cowardice,
Who can't even hold her emotions?
Can't even fight for herself,
Is it really me, am known for ages?
Can't be!
no matter what it takes to "BE ME"
Or to get back on my esteems and ethics
I will not let myself down and degraded
At any cost, even with my life!
My sorrows are admirable,
My pains need exaltation!
Nought to secrete of,
You are stronger than your conjecture!
"Courage, valiance and chivalry,
All you need to subjugate the battle,
Against your antagonist or LIFE!

Believe you and you're going to shine above all!
........whispered stars quietly"

23. Comparison!

Why there is any need to compare
When we all are aware of the fact
That we all are unique,
Unique in our way!
The reason you can't find anyone
Identical to you is that
God has never created
The two apples with similar seeds
Then why the heck this word
"COMPARISON" is still prevalent?

No doubt this word has taken away
So many of the lives!
Every other person on this Earth is
Undergoing with this mental illness!
Illness??
Yes, Eleiyaca Dazura you heard me right!
An illness, which is worse than
the feeling of demise!
This illness subjugates the functionality
Of mind and filled him with all the negativities this world holds!
You know what Eleiyaca,
What does hurt the most
When you've been compared by those
Who are precious to you,
When your parents, friends, and your
Fellow mates
Set the bar limit of expectations
And you failed to live upon,
At that stage the thin line creates
And your loved ones start comparing
Others to you!
Every person on this Earth holds
Unique abilities and capabilities!
You cannot afford to lose yourself
Just for the sake of being somebody,
Somebody who's not even important
More than yourself!
The world is busy in imitating shades
While fading away from their bases!

VANDANA

What on Earth would it take to
Obliterate the ideology of being perfect?
You know what Elie,
I'm undergoing the same agony
Agony in my heart, that never heals
It feels like my heart going to burst out
Someday,
And I would end up doing nothing!
Nought with my life, nought for my life!
I tried my best to make it to the ledge
But every time I accomplish in
Making my dear ones proud
They end up with a new companion
For me, and every time I off to my
bed with the same feeling like I'm
Worthless!
I'm arrogant, choleric, and sullen
But I too have feelings!
I cry, I mourn, I yell every night
With my disappointment and
Disgrace!
That I was failed to live upon
Those expectations made by
glimmering eyes!
"Comparison sucks badly, but
The feeling of hatred and fire
That cradling in your abdomen,
Could create wonders, only if
Used in the right direction!

So, keep that fire alive in your heart
And have faith in you and your plans!
One day you will be successful in
Showing the world your true worth!" Said Eleiyaca.

Part-3: War, loss and death!

24. The night we met!

It's hurting

But what?

I held my head

In my both hands

Slowly opened my eyes

The place was hard to recognize

Brought my hands to my sight

It had blood and bruises on my right

I looked around and the view was dreadful

The broken building and souls were heedful

It took me a moment to be in my senses

This mutiny is led by war consequences

I stood up and looked around

This lifeless land was once

a blooming town

As soon my nerves started working

I ran diagonally tumbling, yet searching

Searching my family in this cemented ground

Hours passed but nothing had been found

I was exhausted and yelling

Blood was oozing through my mouth, dwelling

Till now I had received several injuries

I lost everything but not memories

I lost every hope and

My country lost the war
I was about to fell
But something stopped me well
The next moment I opened my eyes
I was complexed with lies
A man was standing in front of me
I rubbed my eyes hard so that I could see
I was charmed by his enticing smile
though I was suspicious beguile
He sat across my side
I tried to elope but my leg was tied
Tied with a plaster on it
War injuries were unhealed
He was looking at me puzzled
White moon paper and his hands scribbled
The silence was all I could hear
And silence I could not bear
I snapped from the window
It was all dark and dire shadow
Shadow of night
Shadow of plight
My curious mind broke the silence
And asked out of impatience
Where's my family?
All I could hear was silence
And therefore, repeated my sentence
Where's my family?
This time he looked up
Straight into my eyes, but

Lips were still seized
And I was peeved
I broadened my eye shape
That made words escape
And finally, he muttered
"They are dead"!
For an hour, I positioned numb
This was the war outcome
And the price paid by all
On the political call!
He embraced me in his arms
And gave my dying soul warmth!
His arms were so soothing,
I slept and stopped breathing!

"Your breath soothe my pacing heart, your touch give deep chills to my dying heart!"

"Embrace me in your arms,

Halt the eternal time,

Uplift my face with your warm palms,

And plant a kiss like a sunshine!"

25. Her demise!

My best friend and I have always been together,
We supported, laughed and cried all together!
Going to school, with our dusty bicycles,
Myriad remembrances, we recycled!
Her elegance toward animals and,
revolution to save them was sensible!
Our silly gossips had no sense,
But our meaning to life was intense!
Days passed, memories faded,
And that friendship, degraded!
One very fine day,
I was on my way!
And heard a scream,
All I could see was sunbeams!
There was blood all around,
When I reached, I was bound,
I wanted to yell,
But I kept in a shell!
The scent was so familiar,
And the pendant was recognisable!
She was sitting on a chair,
Blood spilt everywhere!
Tears cascaded from my eyes,
Please can you wake up and surprise?

I never wanted to believe,
This overwhelming grieve!
I bow down on my knees,
I was shivering and got freeze!
For the past thirty hours,
I poured my all scars!
My throat got chocked,
My voice croaked!
I exclaimed,
"Oh, my dear!
My favourite peer!
Why you left me,
Can't you see?
You were my happiness,
Reason for my craziness!
Now, what will I do?
Say it isn't true"
While speaking of all,
Tears from her eyes fall!
Her hand touched my cheek,
I got the answers that I seek!
The paper in her hand,
Made my concerns understand!
She was murdered by her husband,
I regretted that I couldn't take her stand!
Reading all she wrote made me amazed,
She was the only soul I most craved!
She had the liveliest vitality,
My my, she was killed with brutality!

VANDANA

Birds were chirping all around
Patting her face with crying sound
Dogs and kitties were sitting
Sorrow in their eyes,
Hoping and waiting!
I wept away my eyes out,
With all my left breath, I shout!
I decided to avenge her,
With all the evidence there were!
With my firm resolve,
I succeeded to solve!
All the mysteries,
Her demise holds!

*****

"Wilted flowers"

26. Insights of war!

A buzzing sound,
Was moving all around!
With a message flash,
Of countries clash!
Declaration of war,
Has pandered the roar!
The city was under an
Open fire,
The situation around was
Vigorously dire!
Bullets were shooting
Everywhere,
People were dying from
Nowhere!
People standing still,
withstanding the injuries,
gallantly upholding!
The announcement was so sudden,
It revealed the hidden!
I could not only hear to fire shots
and Screams,
But also, to shattered visions and
partial dreams!
Military doing its best to protect,

Yet, vulnerable to defend!
It isn't just a war between two
Countries,
But, a ruthless agreement of
people life itineraries!
The heinous act of humanity,
Solely ravage the serenity!
Some lost their beloved,
In the battle of hatred!
Some reported missing,
And some kept bashing!
Innocent children and
Old hags were brutally
banged down,
Artilleries were summoned
In the town!
Severed limbs and wailing voices,
Whimpering eyes and undesirable
Choices!
I, being a soldier of my nation,
Strive for the world's better creation!
Watching my comrades killed in
the battle,
filled my heart with aggression and
Memories were frequently Skedaddle!
To kill or be killed by our enemy,
Is what we share as our destiny!
Within an hour, the city got quiet,
And bodies were lying there in silence!

But fortunately, the country triumph,
Conquering over the enemy's alliance!
But is it a victory?
Or records of history?
With whom the authority will
Celebrate the success?
To whom will show its gratitude
And to whom will address?
The chaos being created,
Left nothing, but hatred!
The pain and agony of those
who lost everything,
Now knows wrath and vengeance
as their primary thing!
Humans aren't easy to comprehend,
And their ravenous wars have no end!
Thus, the blooming town turned to
Desolate cemetery,
And become banausic to mercenary!

27. Will of fire!

People differ by personalities so
Their notion of integrity!
Why do we exist in this cruel world?
Where truth is being depreciated,
And traitors are being appreciated!
Where the meaning of life is obscure,
But the path of darkness is definite!
Facing harsh reality, people
Dying worthless, lost in darkness
Wandering for affection!
For what Almighty has created us
decades ago?
For humanity and to
Defend brotherhood!
On the contrary, we people
Stimulating crises, violence,
Soldering our lips and holding
Back against our livelihood!
We lost our track in darkness
Chasing over petty things,
Humanity is at the Brink of Extinction,
Still, all we care about is the destruction!
We need to wake up,
From our illusions and must

Put our courage together,
To face reality with valiance!
If not we, then who?
If not now, then when?
If not here, then where?
We are no longer scared by
Animals and disasters,
Our only foe is we, humans,
Who poses threat to our
Mankind and evolution!
We live in our fantasy and
call Them reality, where reality
Is what we call nightmares,
Words are mere tools,
Used by hate to make us fools!
Our steps hold many lives,
Go ahead save the tribes!
Rise up again, fall down twice,
WE together have to strike!
The world is waiting for our
Action,
The story has half done,
Now is the time for our reaction!
Things will be cruel
We have to be brutal, but
REMEMBER,
No matter how many situations get dire
Always Keep alive the WILL OF FIRE!!!

28. To our brave-hearts!

Life is a treasure
You can't get a hold,
For them, it's a pleasure
Who are valiant and bold!!
My deep consolation to our great martyrs,
and a big-hearted salute to our brave-hearts!!
Soldiers always armed to protect the nation
They are the most kind and selfless,
Good deeds are their only passion
But when it's about us, they are the most relentless!!
My deep consolation to our great martyrs,
and a big-hearted salute to our brave-hearts!!
They consolidate and leave their houses
To shelter our motherland and strangers,
They crave for their children and spouses
Standing on the border confronting with danger.
My deep consolation to our great martyrs,
and a big-hearted salute to our brave-hearts!!
They endure pain with great fortitude
Their blood has been cherished with chivalrous,
My head always rise in pride and gratitude as,
They never flinch facing the dreadful battle.
My deep consolation to our great martyrs,
and a big-hearted salute to our brave-hearts!!

They need not our fame and glory
Their divine courage is ineffable,
This is a never-ending story
Their journey to live is incredible,
and being a soldier for our country has always been a splendour.
My deep consolation to our great martyrs,
and always an indebted salute to our brave- hearts!!!

A Word Of Gratitude!

Thankyou to all my readers for selecting this book and reading it to the end. This book is nothing without you and I adore my every reader.

If you had any thoughts while or after reading this book, you can anytime share your thoughts and connect with me on my instagram profile @_pileofbooks.